Backyard Birds

Looking Through the Glass

Glen Apseloff

OHIO DISTINCTIVE PUBLISHING

Columbus, Ohio

To my wife, Lucia, who planted seeds for this, both figuratively and literally.

Acknowledgements: Special thanks to my twin brother, Stan, and to my parents and other family members who critiqued this book. Thanks also to the many birds that visited my feeders and that continue to enrich my life.

Text and photographs by Glen Apseloff. All photographs were taken through closed windows from inside a suburban house in the American heartland. No birds were touched or disturbed for any of the photographs.

To inquire about special discounts for bulk purchases, please contact Ohio Distinctive Publishing by email: books@ohio-distinctive.com or by phone: 614-459-3100.

10 9 8 7 6 5 4 3 2 1
012013-1-5000-JO-37040

Printed in the United States of America.

ISBN 978-1-936772-08-7

Library of Congress Control Number: 2012924276

Ohio Distinctive Publishing
6500 Fiesta Drive
Columbus OH 43235
www.ohio-distinctive.com

Every photograph in this book was taken from inside my house (in Powell, Ohio) through a closed window. This in part explains the title: Looking Through the Glass. But the title is intended to mean more than that. For most of my life, I viewed windows as simply something to let in light. I didn't appreciate what was on the other side. I do now.

The title of this book is also a play on words of Lewis Carroll's literary work, and it's a metaphor. When Alice stepped through the looking glass, she entered a place of wonder. When I look through the windows of my house, I too experience that, and when you read this book, I hope the same thing happens to you.

The baseball player Yogi Berra once said, "You can observe a lot just by watching." Until recently, I didn't do that, and I didn't notice much around me. I had no clue how many species of birds could be found in my own backyard, and I didn't know enough to distinguish one from another if they looked even remotely alike. To me, a sparrow was a sparrow. Not a song sparrow or a field sparrow or a house sparrow or a chipping sparrow. Just a sparrow. I had grown up with cardinals in the neighborhood (they're the state bird of Ohio), but I never wondered how a juvenile of that species differed from an adult, or how juveniles of any species differed from adults. I had also never noticed that birds molt, and I never gave any thought to possible differences between winter and summer plumage, let alone the transition between the two. I've since learned the basics, or at least some of them, from books and from the internet, including web sites of state departments of natural resources, the Audubon Society, and the Cornell Lab of Ornithology (www.allaboutbirds.org). The information I provide in this book is from those sources.

Until a couple of years ago, I believed central Ohio was relatively devoid of wildlife. With that misconception in mind, I traveled widely to photograph animals as far away as Madagascar, Botswana, New Zealand, Alaska, and even Antarctica. Usually I hired guides, and they showed me local fauna in natural settings, sometimes with stunning backdrops—the jungle, the ocean and mountains, glaciers. I never imagined that anything in Ohio could compare to that, to lemurs hanging from trees, or penguins jumping off icebergs. Certainly nothing in my own backyard could compare. But then a couple of years ago I faced an extended period without a vacation. As weeks turned into months, and one season into the next, I felt increasingly compelled to take out my camera and photograph something. *Anything.*

That's when I thought of what I might be overlooking. Backyard birds? Maybe, but how many birds can people really see in their own backyard? When I go to art festivals and find photographs of what look like backyard birds, the photographers invariably tell me they took the pictures in a state park or some other out-of-the-way place. Of course, people really do take pictures in their own backyards, but the best photographs I've seen have always been somewhere else.

So what about *my* backyard? Could I photograph anything there? I had serious doubts. Especially in the winter. It isn't like Antarctica where you can just sit down and penguins waddle up to you and peck at your parka.

One thing I knew was that I did not want to spend a lot of time outside in the winter. The last time I did cold-weather photography, I thought I might get frostbite and cause permanent damage to my fingers, despite chemical hand warmers inside my gloves. I don't mind sacrificing time, money, and comfort to photograph wildlife, but I draw the line at body parts.

However, outdoor photography typically takes place outdoors, and if it's done in the winter, that means going out in the cold. Or does it? Instead of photographing birds the way countless other photographers do, by going out and finding them, what if I just stayed inside and waited for the birds to find me?

That's how I came up with the idea for this project. One of my objectives with wildlife photography has always been to give people a better appreciation of nature. By photographing birds from inside my house, I could show others what they're missing around them, and maybe I could motivate them to want to see more and to learn more. I could show people that working long hours and seeing daylight primarily through the windows of an office building or a house isn't an excuse to ignore nature. I could show them that all they have to do is look outside. This was assuming, of course, that I could find birds to photograph.

With that goal in mind, I embarked on this project. It started as a calendar, not a book—a calendar of backyard birds photographed from inside my house, through closed windows. I wasn't sure I could find a dozen different species, but I figured I could include pictures of both males and females for those that are sexually dimorphic, and then I might need as few as half a dozen. Eventually I should be able to find that many.

I used a handheld camera (no tripod or cable release for remote pictures) with no special filters, not even a polarized filter, and no flash. I wanted to show what people can see if they simply look outside their windows. I removed a couple of screens, put up decals to try to minimize the likelihood that birds would fly into the glass, and then I started observing. Because it was winter, with no plants to attract birds, I put out suet and bird seed in feeders on my back deck and experimented with different types. I learned that most birds seemed to prefer peanut-butter suet (especially with large pieces of peanuts) and definitely black-oil sunflower seeds. Many birds were also attracted to safflower seeds, and the smaller birds (including finches, buntings, and chickadees) seemed to prefer a mix of finch food with millet and sunflower seeds.

Like other full-time workers anywhere, I could find only limited opportunities to watch and photograph birds. I've never been good at standing still for extended periods, but I forced myself to spend time at the windows, and not just the ones with a view of the back deck. I began looking out the bathroom windows, the dining-room windows, and even the little panes of glass alongside my front door.

My wife, Lucia, bought a book called *Birds of Ohio Field Guide* by Stan Tekiela, and I looked at the pictures to identify birds I saw outside. When I first flipped through the pages, I couldn't believe such a wide variety of birds lived in Ohio. The book described more than a hundred of them, and in the introduction, the author mentioned that more than 400 different species have been recorded in Ohio. I found that especially difficult to believe. But then, after I started this project, everything changed. I began seeing birds—unusual and even exotic ones—through my windows: brilliant blue indigo buntings and other species that I thought existed only in the tropics, such as the scarlet tanager. I was amazed by how many birds I observed "just by watching." Close to half of them, I had never seen in my life—northern flickers, ruby-throated hummingbirds, cedar waxwings, and a rose-breasted grosbeak, to name a few. Others I had seen but had never really noticed, like the multicolored iridescent European starlings that I had always thought were simply gray and black.

In an attempt to show people what they can see just by looking through their windows, I discovered what I had been missing for years, actually for decades. In this book, I'll show you what that was. I've arranged the birds in alphabetical order by common name (e.g., "bunting, indigo" precedes "robin, American") for lack of a better system. Whenever I introduce a bird, the name is in bold print. The first entry is a blackbird, more specifically a **red-winged blackbird**.

The bird below landed on a plant hanger on my back deck before going to a nearby feeder for sunflower seeds.

Male red-winged blackbird

Male red-winged blackbird

Red-winged blackbirds are common in Ohio and can be found in a variety of places, although they prefer wetlands. Until I began putting out feeders, I never saw one in Ohio and didn't realize they could be seen in this part of the country. The male shown above perched briefly on a tree in a flowerpot on my back deck. Usually I see a few males together (the females are more elusive) on or near the feeders. They seem particularly fond of black-oil sunflower seeds, and sometimes two males crowd a single small feeder meant for finches and buntings.

Red-winged blackbirds can be found throughout the U.S., including Alaska, and their range extends as far south as Costa Rica. Although they are considered year-round residents in most of the U.S., some migrate to southern states during the winter. They are omnivores, and much of their diet consists of seeds, grains, and insects. Flocks vary in size but are much larger in the winter, when they may number in the millions, nearly filling the sky and undulating in surreal displays. These flocks also include starlings and other species of blackbirds. The birds can cause considerable damage to crops, and some farmers illegally kill them with pesticides.

Male red-winged blackbirds are highly territorial and also highly polygynous; they may have more than a dozen females in their territory, although some of those females may mate with other males. The average life expectancy is only about two years in the wild, but one bird was documented to have survived for almost sixteen years.

Female red-winged blackbird

Red-winged blackbirds are highly sexually dimorphic—males and females look nothing alike—and females are sometimes mistaken for sparrows. Their markings provide camouflage that protects the nesting birds from predators.

In flight, males display bright patches of red and yellow on their wings. They also show more of the red as a threat display or in territorial behavior.

Juvenile red-winged blackbird

Juveniles are highly variable in appearance. They may look the same as adult females, but other times they may look like another species. The juvenile above could be mistaken for a European starling. In contrast, **Eastern bluebirds** are unmistakable.

Male Eastern bluebird

Native to Ohio, Eastern bluebirds are also called blue robins; they're the only species of bluebirds with the combination of a blue back and a rust-colored breast. I had never seen one until I put out suet, and now I have so many photographs of them that selecting a dozen images for this book was difficult. I see many more bluebirds in the winter than the summer, presumably because they have better food sources in the warmer months.

Male Eastern bluebird on an artemesia plant

Male Eastern bluebird

In the cold of winter, as shown on the previous page and below, bluebirds frequently fluff their feathers to trap air between the feathers and their body, for added insulation.

Male Eastern bluebird

Male Eastern bluebirds

Female (above) and male Eastern bluebirds

Most of the bluebirds I photographed for this book were relatively skittish. However, I intentionally never used any sort of blind, or anything to conceal myself, because I wanted this to be a true representation of what people can see without making any effort other than simply watching. Many of the birds flew away after only a few seconds, but others became accustomed to seeing me in the window and took as much time as they needed. Occasionally a few would visit my feeders simultaneously, as shown on the next page.

Male Eastern bluebirds perched and a female in flight

Male Eastern bluebird

Female Eastern bluebirds appear more gray than blue, especially the head. Juveniles resemble females but with spotted breasts.

Bluebirds are not nearly as common in Ohio as they were a hundred years ago. The population here declined by as much as ninety percent after the early 1900s, the result of a loss of habitat and competition from house sparrows and European starlings, introduced to the U.S. in the mid and late 1800s. House sparrows and starlings compete with bluebirds for nesting cavities.

Female Eastern bluebird

Female Eastern bluebird

To support bluebirds and other native species, as well as to conserve and create habitats that promote them, the Ohio Bluebird Society was created in 1987. This organization provides a variety of information and recommendations for anyone interested in helping bluebirds (and other native species), including instructions regarding how to create nest boxes, where to put the boxes, and what to feed to the birds.

Female Eastern bluebird

Female Eastern bluebird

Male and female Eastern bluebirds seem to visit my feeders in equal numbers, in contrast to what occurs with red-winged blackbirds. I'm not sure where they come from because I've never seen any nests. My wife put out several bird houses in trees a couple of years ago, but we don't know whether any of them have ever been used.

Indigo buntings are similar to bluebirds around my feeders—I had at first been unaware that they could be found in Ohio, but now I see them frequently. Like bluebirds, most are skittish, but not all. Some ignore me, and a few appear comfortable posing for the camera.

Although male indigo buntings appear to be a brilliant sapphire blue, they are in fact black. They appear blue because of the way their feathers refract light. Cellular structures in the feathers act like a prism and separate the light into different colors instead of simply reflecting it. Some of the separated colors are absorbed, whereas others are reflected back (blue in the case of male indigo buntings). In bright daylight, the blue coloration appears lighter and iridescent, and the feathers take on the appearance of fine hair.

The male pictured below is perched in a lemon tree that my wife grew from a seed and put in a planter on our back deck during the summer. The bird was only ten or twelve feet away and allowed me to photograph it for the better part of a minute.

Male indigo bunting

I discovered by accident that indigo buntings are attracted to finch food, and I subsequently experimented with a few different types. Although finches are especially fond of thistle, the seeds get scattered and as a result, the lawn becomes overgrown with thorny weeds. To avoid that, I tried a variety of other mixes and found that the birds seem to like a combination of sunflower seeds and millet, although I believe they're attracted mainly to the millet.

Male indigo bunting

Male indigo bunting

During the summer months, indigo buntings usually visit my feeders several times per day. Most are territorial, and often they chase larger birds away from a feeder or a nearby tree limb.

Male indigo bunting

Like red-winged blackbirds, indigo buntings are highly sexually dimorphic. Whereas males are almost entirely a brilliant blue, females have only a hint of that coloration in their plumage. At a glance the females appear entirely brown, but a closer examination reveals blue striations near the top of their folded wings and in their tail feathers. Both male and female indigo buntings have an upper beak that appears darker than their lower beak.

Sometimes two indigo buntings perch on the same feeder on my back deck, as shown below, but more frequently one chases the other away. Most of the time when I see two together, they are male and female.

Male indigo buntings

Female indigo bunting

Male indigo bunting molting

Male indigo bunting on a butterfly bush

One bird that I photographed, shown above, would spend hours every day perched on a bush just inches from my dining-room window. It would repeatedly fly up against the glass (not headfirst into it but beating its wings against it), and I've read that this happens when birds see their reflection and try to protect their territory from an apparent intruder. But this bird also flew against screens that should have hidden its reflection. At times the bunting seemed to be trying to get inside the house. Occasionally, as shown below, it would perch on the outside of the window and appear to look through the glass. Usually it flew away if I approached closer than eight or ten feet.

Male indigo bunting perched on a window

I photographed indigo buntings on a variety of plants my wife put on our back deck during the summer. Birds feel more protected with plants around their feeders, especially with larger plants, and they're less likely to fly into windows when the plants are outside.

Female indigo bunting fluffing its feathers

Sometimes indigo buntings fluff their feathers, for example when another bird startles them. I've photographed this in both males and females. A female is shown above.

Unlike indigo buntings, **Northern cardinals** are birds that I've seen throughout my life, although never up close until I put out feeders. They're attracted to both sunflower and safflower seeds. Adult males have brilliant red coloration that rivals that of any tropical birds, and it's especially striking when the cardinals perch on green foliage or snow-covered trees.

Male Northern cardinals in the spring, fall, and winter

Male Northern cardinal

Unlike most other birds, Northern cardinals seem to visit my feeders with similar frequency year round.   Most of them prefer to do that when I'm not standing in the window, and usually they take flight as soon as I approach.

Male Northern cardinal with its crest down

The crest of the birds is down when they're resting, and that's the position in which I typically see it when the birds are around the feeders on my deck. I've taken many hundreds of photographs of cardinals in a variety of settings around my house.

Male Northern cardinal with its crest raised

Sometimes Northern cardinals can be seen with what appears to be a bad-hair day, in which the head feathers are in disarray or appear sparse. Less commonly the birds lose most or all of their head feathers, giving them the appearance of miniature vultures, as shown on the next page. At first I thought this could be the result of trauma, but that's unlikely. Some ornithologists speculate that it's the result of an infection or mites, but others who have examined cardinals without head feathers have found some of the birds to be free of any disease or infestation. The most likely explanation in those cases is simply an unusual molting pattern. Cardinals molt every year, but typically just a few feathers at a time (usually only one feather at a time on their wings, but more on their body and head). Having a bald head isn't only aesthetically displeasing for the cardinals; it also increases the risk of injury. Feathers provide protection from small branches or thorns and from the elements.

Male Northern cardinal with unusual molting pattern

Below is a male cardinal undergoing molting. During this process, the birds fly less to conserve energy, but I see relatively large numbers of them at my feeders, presumably because they find that obtaining the seeds requires minimal effort.

Juvenile male Northern cardinal with irregular molting pattern

Female Northern cardinals have a much duller coloration than males. At a glance they appear to be a rusty orange, but they have red in their crest, wings, and tail. Like males, adult females have orange beaks surrounded by dark feathers, as shown below.

Female Northern cardinal

Many times I've seen male and female cardinals together, and sometimes I see one male chasing another. Usually cardinals eat directly from feeders, but they also eat dropped seeds on the deck or the ground.

Juvenile Northern cardinals are easy to identify because their beaks are black instead of orange. Otherwise they appear similar to females but without red in their crown and with duller coloration in their wings and tail feathers.

Juvenile Northern cardinal molting a feather from its crest

Female Northern cardinal eating a sunflower seed

When cardinals are seen close up, the intricate pattern of the feathers in their crest becomes apparent, as shown above. With good lighting and a bird that isn't far away, this pattern can be seen or photographed fairly easily.

Unlike Northern cardinals, which are readily recognizable, some **chickadees** may be difficult to identify. Distinguishing Carolina chickadees from black-capped chickadees is especially challenging. In general, black-capped chickadees are found in the North, and Carolina chickadees are found in the south. However, they have overlapping ranges, including part of Ohio. In these areas, the birds may hybridize, and telling them apart can be impossible. In areas where hybridization does *not* occur, the differences between the two species have been described as "slight but obvious." The easiest way to differentiate them is by their vocalizations. However, I usually don't hear them from inside my house. Black-capped chickadees have white on their greater coverts (the small feathers that cover the bases of the large feathers on the upper part of the wing) and have a slightly larger black bib. They also have a more pronounced cinnamon coloration on their underparts. The bird below appears to have more characteristics of a black-capped chickadee, whereas the one on the next page appears more characteristic of a Carolina chickadee.

Carolina chickadee or black-capped chickadee on a sunflower

Carolina chickadee or black-capped chickadee

Black-capped chickadees and Carolina chickadees are among the boldest birds I've encountered in Ohio. They're usually the first to visit the feeders that I refill (especially those with safflower seeds), and they rarely appear startled when I come to the window to take pictures. Photographing them is a challenge, however, because of the contrast in their coloration. In most photographs, either the black part of their head is underexposed or the white is overexposed. The best images are obtained on cloudy days.

In contrast to chickadees, **brown-headed cowbirds** are unwelcome at many bird feeders. Makers of bird seed often advertise that their blend does not attract this species. Most of these birds seem skittish around the feeders I put out, perhaps because people frequently shoo them away. Brown-headed cowbirds have a negative reputation in large part because they lay their eggs in the nests of other birds, and many of those other birds nurture the chicks.

Brown-headed cowbirds can lay dozens of eggs in a season, and they're not particular about where they do it, including the nests of raptors and even hummingbirds. Interestingly, brown-headed cowbirds have been observed checking on their eggs and their young in other birds' nests.

Like indigo buntings, brown-headed cowbirds are highly sexually dimorphic. Females at a slight distance appear to be a drab grayish brown, whereas males are a dark iridescent blue (sometimes with purple hues) with a brown head. In the sunlight the upper breast may appear purple and the head a rich mahogany. Juveniles may look more like females but vary considerably and are sometimes difficult to identify.

Male brown-headed cowbird

Male brown-headed cowbird

Female brown-headed cowbird

Female brown-headed cowbird

Around my house, **crows** appear even more cautious than brown-headed cowbirds; they rarely if ever visit my feeders. Briefly one perched on a post of my back deck, just long enough for me to take the photograph below.

American crow

I see crows frequently in my neighborhood and along the streets I drive to work. Highly intelligent, they understand the movement of cars and the basic rules of traffic lights. They're considered more capable than many primates in solving problems that require multiple steps (e.g., figuring out how to obtain a short stick, then using the short stick to solve another problem to obtain a longer stick, then using the longer stick as a tool to retrieve food from an enclosure). They can be easily trained but are unappealing to most people as pets simply because they are black.

Crows have complex and effective methods of communication, and they have excellent memories. They can be taught to talk like parrots and can imitate other animals. A myth has been circulated that their tongue needs to be split in order for them to talk, and this misinformation has led some people to inflict a cruel surgical procedure on captive birds.

The visual acuity of crows is excellent, and these birds are also able to distinguish human faces. These attributes, coupled with the fact that the birds are intelligent and trainable, have inspired researchers to investigate the possibility of using crows for search and rescue missions to locate individuals lost in a desert.

Crows are disliked by some people not only because of their appearance but also because they like to collect shiny objects for their nests; they may steal items of value and have been known to damage transformers when they incorporate wire coat hangers into nests they build on utility poles. This is a significant problem in large cities in Japan, where people routinely use wire coat hangers to dry clothing outdoors.

Like crows, **mourning doves** are common birds. However, they are infrequent visitors to feeders, instead preferring to eat seeds that have dropped to the ground. The one below landed on an iron plant hanger roughly ten feet from where I was standing.

Mourning dove

Mourning doves have only recently been coming to my deck with any frequency. They sometimes visit a small platform feeder on which I put black-oil sunflower seeds and safflower seeds.

Mourning doves

Mourning dove

On the platform feeder I put out, mourning doves always seem accommodating of other birds; I've never seen them behave in a territorial manner, and I frequently see them sharing the seeds with much smaller birds, including finches and chickadees. When they're ground feeding, they sometimes come within a few feet of where I'm standing at the window if I don't make any sudden movements.

The name "mourning dove" originates from the mournful cooing sounds the birds make. At first glance, these doves appear to be just plain tan with some dark markings, but they have small multicolored iridescent patches on their necks. The striations of their feathers also create an intricate pattern, as shown in the photographs above and on the next page. Mourning doves are among the more visually appealing birds I've photographed. From inside my house I've photographed them in trees, in flight, and also in the act of mating (shown below).

Mourning doves mating

Male and female mourning doves look alike, although males tend to be larger. I've read that males also have a blue-gray area on the nape of their neck and a faint pink coloration that shimmers on their neck.

Mourning dove

Mourning doves are monogamous, and they have the longest lifespan of any terrestrial bird in North America. One tagged dove was documented to have lived more than thirty-one years in the wild. Although protected under U.S. law by the Federal Migratory Bird Treaty Act, the Act permits managed hunting established by individual states. As a result, mourning doves are the most frequently hunted species of birds in the U.S., with more than 20 million shot annually. In Ohio, one of the forty states that permits hunting, the life expectancy of these birds is only one and a half years, and the majority of mourning doves do not survive from one year to the next.

Like mourning doves, **house finches** are common in Central Ohio. Males have an overall red coloration, but occasionally they're yellow or orange. The variation in coloration is the result of different diets during molting, and the intensity of their color may vary from one season to the next. A typical diet high in carotenoids produces red coloration. Variations in the pattern of colors occur among different subspecies.

Females are brown with white markings on their breast. Frequently males and females are seen together. They have a reputation for being gregarious, and several at a time often visit a single feeder. Although native to the U.S., the birds are not native to Ohio. They were originally confined to the western states but were released into the wild in New York in the 1940s and have since spread throughout the country.

Male house finch

Male and female house finch

Male house finch

Male house finch fluffing its feathers

Male house finch resting with feathers fluffed

Yellow male house finch

Above is a yellow male house finch, one of only two that I have photographed. I've also photographed an orange male. The extent of the coloration is highly variable. Some males look similar to purple finches, with deep red extending over their head and covering much of their body. However, purple finches typically lack the dark streaks on their flanks, and they have a beak that's more conical (the culmen, or top of the upper bill, is relatively straight rather than curved).

Female house finch fluffing its feathers

House finches are among the most photographed birds I have in my collection for this project, and selecting the images for this book was difficult. The birds seem at times coy, inquisitive, playful, and petulant. They usually allow me several seconds to take a photograph before they hop off a perch and fly away.

In contrast to house finches, **Northern flickers** are a species I never encountered until I put out food for them. They're migratory but can be seen year round in Ohio. They visit my suet feeders primarily in the winter, when food is scarce. Usually I see isolated birds.   Males and females look similar, but males have a black mustachelike marking on both cheeks.

Male Northern flicker

Female Northern flicker

Ohio is home to yellow-shafted Northern flickers, whereas red-shafted Northern flickers are found in the West. The western birds have red instead of black mustaches. The names "yellow-shafted" and "red-shafted" refer to the color underneath their wings, observed when they're in flight.

Male American goldfinch in summer plumage

American goldfinches, also called wild canaries, are relatively common in Central Ohio. They're attracted to thistle, and they visit feeders year round. In late spring they sometimes eat fruit off the service berry outside my dining-room window, as shown above. They're also frequent visitors to my finch feeder.

Males in their summer plumage can be challenging to photograph because of the contrast between their black and bright yellow coloration. They're easiest to photograph on cloudy days. Their yellow coloration in summer plumage is the result of carotenoids in their diet during the spring when they are replacing molted feathers.

Males in the winter lose the black patch on their forehead, and their bright yellow plumage changes to dull brown. They can be differentiated from females during this time in part by the color of their wings. Females have dark gray markings, whereas the corresponding parts on males are jet black. In the winter the color of the beak of both males and females changes from orange to black.

Male American goldfinch completing its molt into summer plumage

Male American goldfinch in winter plumage

Female American goldfinch

Females in the summer differ significantly from males. They lack the males' black forehead, and their coloration is relatively dull, a mix of yellow and gray. Juvenile males appear similar to females until their second summer.

Male birds that change plumage from one season to the next, such as the American goldfinch, typically display bright colors to attract females during the breeding season and then dull colors to make them less noticeable to predators during periods of nonbreeding.

The **bronzed grackle** is a subspecies of common grackle found in Ohio. Males and females are similar. They're ground feeders that frequent the lawns in my neighborhood, but I have seen only one on my deck. The bird didn't eat anything, but it posed briefly for my camera. Common grackles are omnivores but have a fondness for corn. They live year round in Ohio. Grackles are blackbirds, and in the shade they appear black or dark blue, but in sunlight their head turns an iridescent blue and their body turns an iridescent bronze, like the opposite of a brown-headed cowbird. Shown on the next page are photographs of the same bird in different light.

Bronzed grackle

Bronzed grackle in subdued light

Bronzed grackle in bright sunlight

The **rose-breasted grosbeak** is another example of a bird that I have seen only once on my deck. Early one evening I was standing at the window watching the feeders on the back deck, when this black-headed, white-breasted bird with a patch of bright red in the center of its breast landed on a plant hanger approximately ten feet from me where I had hung a suet feeder. It ate the suet for more than half a minute and then flew away. I have never seen one since, although they're supposed to be common birds.

Male rose-breasted grosbeak

Female rose-breasted grosbeaks look nothing like males. They're drab and can be confused with sparrows, although they have a white stripe above their eyes. On one occasion I spotted a female on the ground eating dropped seeds, but it flew away before I could photograph it.

Cooper's hawk

Cooper's hawks are common in Ohio and are difficult to differentiate from sharp-shinned hawks, also found in Ohio. Cooper's hawks have a wingspan of 27 to 36 inches (females are larger than males). They're also called bird hawks because their diet consists primarily of small birds. These hawks are more likely than other raptors to attack birds at backyard feeders. Twice they've landed on my back deck within ten feet of where I was standing behind the window, but both times they flew off only an instant later. One of those times I managed to turn my camera on the hawk, but the raptor moved faster than my lens could focus.

Both times the hawks landed on my deck, they failed to catch any birds. They rely on the element of surprise, but that frequently doesn't work well for them. Occasionally I spot them in trees near my house, but usually other birds spot them first. I know they're in the area when all the other birds, squirrels, and chipmunks suddenly disappear. This hawk in the photograph above was perched in a tree not far from my deck, but flurries obscured much of the detail in the image.

Cooper's hawks are monogamous. They build nests together and usually mate for life. Males are typically submissive to females.

Male ruby-throated hummingbird

Until recently I had never seen a Cooper's hawk, and I had also never seen a **ruby-throated hummingbird**. My wife planted a honeysuckle bush not far from one side of the house, and I was able to photograph hummingbirds as they hovered over the flowers. Numerous people have told me that the birds readily come to hummingbird feeders, but not on my back deck. The feeders I put out seem to attract only ants.

Male ruby-throated hummingbirds have a bright iridescent red gorget (throat patch), but it actually isn't red at all. It's black. The shimmering effect is created by a combination of refracted light (a prism effect described earlier when I explained why indigo buntings appear blue) and melanin—the black pigment. In addition to creating color, melanin has been reported to add strength to feathers. Some white birds have black feathers on their wing tips, and this may be because that area is subject to the most stress.

Melanins produce colors ranging from black to pale yellow, carotenoids produce red, and porphyrins produce pink, red, brown, and green. No pigment in birds produces blue. Any blue pigments in their diet (e.g., blueberries) are destroyed in the digestive tract.

In contrast to males, female hummingbirds have a white throat, shown in the second picture below.

Male ruby-throated hummingbird in shadows, not refracting light

Female ruby-throated hummingbird

Like hummingbirds, **blue jays** refract sunlight to create their coloration, but their color doesn't shimmer because the light doesn't interact with melanin. The lack of blue pigment in the feathers of "blue" birds is evident if you shine a light through the back of a feather instead of the front.

Male and female blue jays look alike, but juveniles have a duller and grayer coloration. Like cardinals, blue jays can sometimes have unusual molting patterns that make them appear bald.

When I first started feeding birds, I rarely saw blue jays, and those that spotted me flew away. Most likely they had learned to be wary of people. They're considered aggressive and generally undesirable because they have been known to eat the eggs and chicks of other birds, but they're primarily vegetarians. They also help other birds by alerting them to predators, and sometimes they chase owls and hawks. In addition, they have been considered instrumental in spreading the growth of oak trees because of their predilection for acorns—a single bird may cache several hundred during the fall.

Blue jay

Blue jay

Juvenile blue jay

Blue jays are related to crows, and like crows, they're curious and intelligent. A neighbor told me that he attracts them with raw peanuts in the shell. I tried that, and they now eat not only the peanuts but also the peanut-butter suet I put out to attract woodpeckers.

Blue jay fluffing its feathers

Blue jays raise their crest when agitated, and occasionally also fluff their feathers, as shown above. They sometimes do this in cold weather to trap air for warmth, and the fine feathers look like strands of hair.

Dark-eyed junco with artemesia plants

Dark-eyed juncos are frequent visitors to my back deck during the winter months only. During the summer, they migrate north out of Ohio into Canada, where their range extends above the Arctic Circle. In many other states, however, they can be spotted year round, especially in the western and northeastern U.S.

Around my house dark-eyed juncos usually feed on dropped finch food rather than directly from feeders. Males tend to be darker than females; females have more brown or a paler black in their plumage. Males can be challenging to photograph in the snow and in bright sunlight because of the contrast between white and black.

Dark-eyed juncos are actually a type of sparrow. They're among the most numerous birds in North America, with a population estimated at more than 600 million, although they form flocks of only up to a few dozen. Because they frequent feeders in the winter, they're often referred to as "snowbirds." The life expectancy of those that survive to fledge is approximately three years.

Dark-eyed junco on a juniper

Like dark-eyed juncos, **red-breasted nuthatches** migrate north out of Ohio in the summer. They're considered common, but I never saw one until after I finished the first draft of this book. Females have a gray cap instead of black, their eyestripe is not as dark as a male's, and their breast is not as red. Juveniles look similar to adults but part of their bill is yellow. Late one Sunday afternoon in mid-October this male visited my deck and ate black-oil sunflower seeds.

Male red-breasted nuthatch

Male red-breasted nuthatch

Male red-breasted nuthatch

White-breasted nuthatches are larger than red-breasted nuthatches and are frequent year-round visitors at my feeders. Often they can be seen head down, even on suet feeders. On my back deck, they sometimes come within a couple of feet of me when I'm standing at the window.

White-breasted nuthatch

White-breasted nuthatch

Like white-breasted nuthatches, **American robins** (below) are abundant in Ohio, but they aren't attracted to bird seed. Instead they prefer earthworms, caterpillars, and grubs. They also eat berries and fruit.

American robin

American robin

American robin

I've read that robins may visit feeders in large numbers if raisins and fresh or frozen berries and cherries are set out for them. I've tried that only a few times and haven't had any success. Rarely a robin will visit my deck apparently just out of curiosity, usually for only several seconds. However, I was fortunate enough one year to have a pair of them nest in the rafters of the underside of the deck. I didn't have adequate lighting to obtain a clear photograph, and I didn't want to use a flash and risk startling the birds, so I settled for the grainy picture below. I took many photographs over a period of many days, but the lighting was never adequate. As I mentioned previously, I didn't use a flash to photograph any of the birds in this book.

American robins

Robins are one of the first species of migratory birds to lay eggs—three to five per nest—in the spring. Nests are built by females without the help of males, and eggs are also incubated without the help of males. Eggs hatch in two weeks, and the chicks leave the nest in another two weeks, although at that point they can fly for only a short distance. They require an additional two weeks before they can sustain a flight. Only one in four birds survives the first year. The average lifespan of a robin is two years, but they have lived for close to fourteen years in the wild and more than seventeen years in captivity.

Some robins are carriers of West Nile virus and can transmit the disease to humans via mosquitos (a mosquito bites an infected robin and then a human).

American tree sparrows are sometimes called "winter chippies" because they look similar to chipping sparrows (described on the next page). American tree sparrows have a brown eye streak instead of black, and they have a two-toned beak—dark upper and yellowish lower. Many of them also have a dark spot in the center of their breast.

American tree sparrow

American tree sparrow

Tree sparrows are found in Ohio only during the winter, and despite their name, they are usually ground feeders and ground nesters. They eat seeds in the winter, and berries and insects when available. They are frequent visitors to feeders in the winter and usually can't survive for more than a day without food.

Unlike American tree sparrows, **chipping sparrows** are summer residents of Ohio. They more often feed on dropped seeds than directly from feeders, and they sometimes hop to within a foot or two of the window where I'm standing.

Males and females look alike, but they both have variable plumage. Breeding plumage is characterized by a bright reddish-brown cap, a white supercilium (the thick line above the eye, running from the base of the beak to the neck), and a black eye streak, whereas nonbreeding adults have a supercilium that is less prominent and a cap that is a mix of black and brown. Younger birds have less brown in their cap.

Males don't help females gather material or build a nest, but they do stand guard. The nests are so flimsy that one can see through them.

Female chipping sparrow gathering material for a nest

72

Chipping sparrow with nonbreeding plumage

Field sparrows are common birds that frequent pastures with weeds and bushes. They have a pink beak, in contrast to the dark beak of the chipping sparrow, and a white eye ring. Their breast is plain except for juveniles, which have streaks. Juveniles also have duller coloration.

Field sparrow

Juvenile field sparrow

Like other sparrows, field sparrows are predominantly ground-feeding seed eaters. Males and females look alike. These birds are known for faking an injured wing to draw the attention of predators away from their chicks.

Although these birds are still considered common, their population across the country has declined by more than half in the past forty years. Researchers speculate that loss of habitat, use of pesticides, introduction of invasive species, and global warming all play a role.

In contrast, **house sparrows** are thriving in the U.S, although they aren't native to this country. They were introduced here in the mid 1800s. Ironically their population is declining in many of their native regions. They prefer to live in areas with people and often nest in the eaves of houses. They are sufficiently comfortable around people that they can sometimes be hand fed. In addition to seeds, grains, and fruit, they eat insects and have been known to pick insects out of the grills of cars.

Male house sparrow in breeding plumage

House sparrows are stockier than other sparrows in North America and have a relatively large head and a stout bill. Nonbreeding adult males have a beak that's yellowish at the base and darker toward the tip, and they have less black on their throat and breast. Females are duller and have a lighter beak. Although these birds are frequent visitors to backyard feeders, I seldom see them where I live.

Song sparrow

Song sparrows are year-round residents in Ohio. Although males and females look alike, the birds are highly variable from one region to the next. In most regions their breast is darkly streaked with a larger mark in the center. In the South and in desert regions they are paler than in the north and in costal regions.

White-throated sparrow

White-throated sparrows are easy to identify because of the yellow marking on their lores (the area between their eyes and their bill), above a black eye stripe. They also have a white throat patch. A variety of these birds has tan and dark brown stripes instead of black and white and may have a dark spot on the breast that might cause a birdwatcher to confuse it for a song sparrow. White-throated sparrows are sometimes mistaken for white-crowned sparrows, although the white-crowned sparrows lack the yellow marking on the lores and also lack a white throat patch.

European starlings are intelligent, highly social birds. They were introduced to this country in 1890 by the Acclimatization Society— William Shakespeare enthusiasts who also introduced house sparrows. Members of this society were intent on bringing to the U.S. every bird mentioned in Shakespeare's writings. Their original introduction of 100 European starlings in New York City's Central Park has grown to 200 million or more throughout North America. According to a *Scientific American* article, Eugene Schieffelin, a New York drug manufacturer, was largely responsible for the introduction of these birds in the U.S.

European starlings are considered an invasive species according to the U.S. Department of Agriculture web site and have contributed to the decline of the Eastern bluebird, but they aid significantly in pest control, consuming large numbers of destructive beetles, cutworms, and other insects. Flocks in the United Kingdom number up to 50,000, and in Denmark have exceeded a million.

European starling in winter plumage

European starlings are among the most colorful birds I've photographed. Until I saw them up close, I had always thought they were gray. In the winter they're a mix of purple, green, yellowish brown, blue, black, and white. Depending on their diet and the time of year, their bill may be dark gray or yellow. Usually I see them at a distance in flocks, but in the winter they come to my suet feeders. In the summer their white spots disappear and the birds have a more glossy appearance. Juveniles appear a dull grayish brown with a black bill, and they can be mistaken for a female brown-headed cowbird, but starlings have a shorter tail. When the juveniles begin to molt into adult plumage, they may take on a striking mix with the colors of a juvenile head but an adult body.

European starling in winter plumage

One of the most brightly colored birds in Ohio is the male **scarlet tanager** in breeding plumage, shown below. Although relatively common in Ohio, these birds are seldom seen because they prefer large forested areas and they forage high in trees, often in oak trees, where they're likely to breed and nest.

Male scarlet tanager

Most male scarlet tanagers in breeding plumage are bright red with black wings, but they can vary in hue and are sometimes orange, like the one I photographed. I was taking pictures of an indigo bunting on a feeder when the tanager lighted on a lemon tree my wife and I had put out onto the deck for the summer. These birds don't normally come to feeders, but it stayed on my deck for nearly a minute. Despite that, poor lighting prevented me from obtaining an optimal image.

The bird was unafraid of me and even stood briefly on the cover of the outdoor grill just a few feet away from me, as shown below, so close I needed to shorten the focal length of my lens to less than 300 mm to get the entire bird to fit optimally in the frame.

Male scarlet tanager

Scarlet tanagers migrate to South America in the winter. Females have an olive-colored back and yellow underside, and males in nonbreeding plumage (in the winter) are olive colored instead of red. In the spring and fall, molting males appear to be a mix of olive and red. Juveniles look like adult females.

In contrast to the male scarlet tanager, the **brown thrasher** has a drab tan coloration and blends into a background of brush. It is the state bird of Georgia and can be seen there year round, but in Ohio it can be found only during the summer. The one I photographed below is the only brown thrasher I've seen anywhere. It stayed on the feeder for perhaps thirty seconds and then flew away.

Brown thrasher

Brown thrashers can be identified by their long tail, the teardrop-shaped markings on their breast, and their bright yellow eyes. Males and females look alike, and juveniles resemble adults except that their eyes are olive or gray.

According to *Cruickshank's Photographs of Birds of America*, brown thrashers have more vertebrae in their neck than giraffes and camels. That information has been repeated on many web sites, but, although correct, it isn't surprising. Giraffes and camels—like humans, bats, and other mammals—have only seven vertebrae, whereas birds have at least eleven, and some, including swans, have as many as twenty-five. More interesting is the fact that brown thrashers have the largest known song repertoire of any bird in North America, up to 3000 by some counts. This is in contrast to the song sparrow, which has a dozen or fewer, or the cedar waxwing, which has none; it is literally a songbird without a song.

Brown thrasher

Brown thrashers are typically ground feeders. They're omnivores and will eat insects, worms, and other invertebrates in addition to fruit, nuts, and seeds.

In contrast to the brown thrasher, the most frequent visitor to my feeders is probably the **tufted titmouse**. From my feeders, they eat sunflower seeds, safflower seeds, suet, and raw peanuts in shells. Sometimes they pick up a peanut shell by the residual stem, but more often they put their beak around the middle of the shell.

Tufted titmouse fluffing its feathers

The tufted titmouse is black, white, gray, and brown, a relatively plain bird at a distance, but up close the striations in the feathers of its crest form an intricate pattern. Most of the birds I've seen have a thin black eye ring that isn't readily apparent because the eyes are also black, but juveniles have a yellow eye ring, as shown in the photograph below.

Juvenile tufted titmouse

Juveniles also have yellow gape flanges, not readily visible on the above photograph. Gape flanges are the area at the base of the upper and lower bill (the corners of the mouth). The coloration in this area is believed to induce the parents of the chicks to feed them.

Tufted titmouse

Tufted titmice are not migratory and can be seen year round in Ohio. Banded birds have been documented to live up to thirteen years in the wild, although the average lifespan is about two years. Most of these birds stay within a few kilometers of where they were hatched.

Tufted titmouse after a rainfall

Most people are probably aware that the "tufted" part of the name of this bird comes from the tuft of feathers on its head, but the origin of "titmouse" is less straightforward. The second syllable actually has nothing to do with mice. The name "titmouse" is derived from the Middle English word "titmose," and the second syllable was originally "māse" in Old English. The Old English word "māse" means "little" or "tiny." Similarly "tit" means "small." Therefore, the name "titmouse" means "small little." These birds look especially small when they pick up a peanut, as shown below.

Tufted titmouse

In the photograph above, note the brown coloration under the wing. That is usually absent in juveniles. Unlike many birds in Ohio, males and females are indistinguishable.

Tufted titmice are known for lining their nests with hair from live animals, and sometimes they pluck hair from dogs. These birds live in pairs rather than flocks, and they build their nests in natural hollows of trees (dead or alive) or in holes created by other birds, often woodpeckers. Their eggs are about the size of a dime.

Tufted titmice eat small invertebrates (insects, caterpillars, spiders, and snails) from spring to fall, in addition to a variety of grains and seeds.   In the fall and winter, they cache food in different places within their territory to eat during severe weather.

Tufted titmouse

Over the past couple of years, I obtained a wide variety of photographs of tufted titmice.   In contrast, I took only a few acceptable photographs of **cedar waxwings**.   I've seen this bird only twice, and the two photographs below are from each of those occasions, separated by one year. The photographs were both taken in the spring, when the service berry just outside my dining-room window bore fruit. This same tree attracts American goldfinch and chipmunks.

Each time I photographed the cedar waxwings below, they flew away within seconds. These birds are considered common in Ohio, year round, even though I had no idea they existed until my wife bought me the Ohio field guide by Stan Tekiela. Cedar waxwings usually have what appear like bright red wax droplets at the tips of their secondary wing feathers, not visible in the photographs below. They also have bright yellow tips on their tail feathers, shown below. They're especially fond of berries, and I've read that when a branch has a cluster only in one place, several birds will sometimes line up and pass berries down the row along the branch so that all of them can eat.

Cedar waxwing

Cedar waxwings are considered songbirds because they belong to the subclass Oscines; "Oscines" is derived from the Latin "oscen" meaning "a songbird." However, cedar waxwings don't sing; they only call. The difference between a song and a call is that a song is usually produced by a male and is usually related to territory and breeding, whereas a call is a simpler, practical, unmusical, and nonsexual utterance to influence or coordinate behavior with other birds. For example, calls may include warnings to alert other birds, communications to indicate location, or protests to drive away intruders.

Cedar waxwing

A variety of woodpeckers visit the suet feeders on my back deck, and they all seem to prefer suet containing large pieces of peanuts. Most often I use suet that is a blend of rendered beef suet, peanuts, peanut meal, and cracked corn, but a variety of different types are made specifically to attract woodpeckers.

Downy woodpeckers are the most frequent visitors to my suet feeders, and sometimes two will perch on a feeder at the same time. They have a long white patch in the center of a black back, shown below on the bird on the left. Males have a small red patch on the back of their head, shown in subsequent photographs. Otherwise males and females look alike. Juveniles appear similar to adults but have red feathers that extend over their crown, as shown below on the bird to the right.

Downy woodpeckers have a characteristic hopping motion that is easy to spot at a distance on trees, even though the birds are small. They are frequently mistaken for their larger cousin, the hairy woodpecker.

Female (left) and juvenile downy woodpeckers

Male downy woodpecker

Juvenile downy woodpecker

The **hairy woodpecker** (shown on the next page) looks almost identical to the downy woodpecker, but the former is roughly fifty percent larger, has a longer bill (more than half as long as the diameter of its head), and has no black spots on its tail. Like downy woodpeckers, males have a patch of red feathers on the back of their head.

Male hairy woodpecker

The **pileated woodpecker** is the largest bird that has ever eaten from any of my suet feeders. These birds commonly exceed one and a half feet in length and can have a wingspan of thirty inches. Males and females appear similar except that males have a red mustache and their red crest begins at the base of their bill, whereas the crest of the females begins farther back on the head. Juveniles have duller red feathers in their crest. I see pileated woodpeckers year round, although only infrequently.

Male pileated woodpecker

Pileated woodpeckers prefer carpenter ants but also eat termites and a variety of other insects, as well as fruits, nuts, berries, and even poison ivy. They seek out large dead trees for creating hollows in which to build nests. They line the nests with wood chips left over from the excavation. Although the entrance to their hollow is only three to four inches in diameter, the excavation may be as deep as two feet, and these birds have been known to break small trees in half by creating too large a hole.

Sizable dead trees are important for pileated woodpeckers not only in building a nest but also for providing food. These trees harbor a large insect population, especially carpenter ants, that the pileated woodpeckers rely upon for sustenance.

Male pileated woodpecker

Male pileated woodpecker

Pileated woodpeckers build a new nest each year, and the abandoned one may become a home for other birds or mammals, including raccoons. I do have raccoons regularly visit my feeders, but I've never been able to locate their dens. Possibly they use the abandoned nests of the pileated woodpeckers.

Pileated woodpeckers have large territories, extending up to 4000 acres, and they defend their territories year round. Rarely are more than two adult birds seen together.

Female pileated woodpecker

Many people have speculated that pileated woodpeckers were the inspiration for the cartoon character Woody Woodpecker, created in 1940. Although the cartoon character much more closely resembles a pileated woodpecker than an acorn woodpecker (not found in Ohio), the latter was the inspiration for the cartoon character, according to National Public Radio and other sources.

In contrast to pileated woodpeckers, **red-bellied woodpeckers** are much more frequent visitors to the suet feeders on my back deck. Males and females look similar except the females have an expanse of gray that interrupts the red coloration of the crown of their head. Females also have a less extensive area of reddish coloration in the feathers on their belly. Otherwise the sexes appear identical. Their backs are covered with black and white barred patterns that have sometimes been compared to the stripes on zebras.

Male (foreground) and female red-bellied woodpeckers

Shown above are a male and female side by side. Although the female is out of focus, the difference between the two sexes is clear, especially the coloration of the head. This is the only time that I have seen two red-bellied woodpeckers together on my deck.

Red-bellied woodpeckers can be found as far north as southern Canada and as far south as Florida. Some of those in the northern part of their range will migrate during the winter, but in Ohio the birds can be found year round. They seem to prefer a suet mix with large pieces of peanuts, and frequently they'll peck at a suet plug until they can extract a large piece.

On rare occasions I've seen them fluff their feathers, as shown in the last photograph in the series that follows.

Male red-bellied woodpecker

Male red-bellied woodpecker

Female red-bellied woodpecker

Juvenile red-bellied woodpecker

Male red-bellied woodpecker

Male red-bellied woodpecker fluffing its feathers

Carolina wrens, the state bird of South Carolina, can be seen year round in Central Ohio, although they cannot survive in harsh winters. They visit my feeders less frequently than most other birds and mainly in the winter. Usually they eat dropped finch food from my back deck. They're easy to spot at a distance because of the sharp angle at which their tail usually juts upward. That isn't shown in the photograph below, but it's readily apparent when the bird is scavenging for food.

Male and female Carolina wrens look alike. Juveniles have paler bellies than adults but otherwise appear identical

Carolina wren

Carolina wren

Other Backyard Animals Photographed Through Windows

In addition to birds, a variety of other wildlife can be seen from indoors. Where I live, I can find everything from insects to deer. Below and on subsequent pages are photographs of various butterflies, all taken through the dining-room window of my house. These insects are attracted to butterfly bushes (an invasive species, shown below) and a variety of other flowers.

American lady butterfly

Female cabbage white butterfly

The **cabbage white butterfly**, shown above, is not native to the U.S. Imported from Europe in approximately 1860, it has one of the longest seasons of any butterfly and competes with native white (Pieris marginalis) butterflies. Cabbage white butterflies measure only about two inches across with their wings open. Males and females are easy to differentiate because males have only one black spot on their wings, instead of two.

The best place to look for butterflies is a flower garden, and the best time is on a calm sunny day. Butterflies seek shelter on overcast days, to escape the threat of rain, and are less likely to visit flowering plants during that time. My wife puts out butterfly houses, but I don't know whether any butterflies have ever used them.

Eastern tiger swallowtail

Eastern tiger swallowtails are common in Ohio. Males are always yellow, but females may be either yellow or dark (almost black).

Peck's skipper butterfly

Silver-spotted skipper

Viceroy butterfly

The **viceroy butterfly** shown on the previous page may be easily mistaken for a monarch butterfly, but monarchs are typically larger and do not have a dark line crossing the veins in their hind wings.

Eastern chipmunks are common visitors to bird feeders. They're considered a nuisance by many people and are sometimes exterminated by trapping and shooting. My wife and I have a large family of them living in our yard under our back deck. When I put out sunflower seeds, the chipmunks stuff their cheek pouches with seeds and then scurry off to cache the food around the yard. As a result, during the late summer we have sunflowers growing in random places in our yard, and even occasionally in a flowerpot. Chipmunks will sometimes dig up roots and bulbs from flowerpots and in their place bury sunflower seeds.

Chipmunks are most active in the mornings and late afternoons. Their range is relatively small, only half an acre or less, and they defend their territory for only about fifty feet around the entrance to their burrow.

Eastern chipmunk on a patio chair

Eastern chipmunk with sunflower seeds

Chipmunks can live for as long as eight years in the wild, but few survive past the age of three. They hibernate in the winter but not continuously like bears. During their hibernation, they eat food stored in their burrow.

Eastern chipmunk in a flowerpot

As shown above, the cheek pouches of chipmunks are considerably large. Recently I watched a chipmunk try to fit two peanuts shells (two peanuts in each shell) into its mouth at the same time. Unfortunately he was facing away from my camera at the time.

White-tailed deer visit my backyard almost every day to eat cracked corn that I put in a feeder. They are the state mammal of Ohio. The state tree (the buckeye) was named after the resemblance of its fruit to the eye of a buck.

According to the web site of the Ohio Department of Natural Resources (ODNR), approximately 500,000 people hunt deer in Ohio. This generates significant revenue from licenses and related fees. However, the entire population of white-tailed deer in Ohio was eliminated in the early 1900s because of overhunting. During the 1920s and 1930s the deer were reintroduced, and in 1943 hunting was again permitted, although with more restrictions.

According to the Division of Wildlife of the ODNR, more than half a million deer were killed in Ohio during the combined 2009-10 and 2010-11 hunting seasons. The 2011 fall herd size in Ohio (at the beginning of the hunting season) was estimated at 725,000.

White-tailed deer can live up to fifteen years, but their average lifespan in the wild is two years for males and three for females. In captivity they have lived up to twenty years.

White-tailed doe and fawn

Hummingbird moths (also called hummingbird clearwing moths or common clearwings) are members of the sphinx moth family and are occasionally mistaken for hummingbirds. They grow up to two inches in length, hover just like hummingbirds, and feed on nectar just like hummingbirds. However, they have a proboscis instead of a beak, prominent antennae, wings that are mostly clear, and six legs instead of two. Their body is olive green with bands of red around their lower body and with red coloration on their wings. They start their life as hornworms—large caterpillars with a flexible hornlike appendage at the hind end.

Unlike most moths that come out at night, hummingbird moths are commonly seen on sunny days. After reaching maturity, these moths can live for up to two years.

Hummingbird moth

Virginia opossums (usually referred to as simply "opossums") eat sunflower seeds that I put out for the birds. They're omnivores and will consume everything from pet food to road kill, although their favorite foods include fruits. Opossums are the only marsupials native to North America and should not to be confused with possums, which are different animals, although also marsupials. Virginia opossums spend the first two to three months of their life nursing in their mother's pouch (after crawling there as embryos); then they cling to her back for another two to three months. At maturity they're roughly the size of a housecat. They have a ratlike prehensile tail that aids in climbing, although it isn't strong enough to hold an adult's entire weight.

Opossums have a reputation for pretending to be dead when confronted by a predator, but in actuality they're simply prone to fainting when subjected to stress. A fainting spell may last for hours, during which the animal's eyes remain fully or partially closed, its mouth foams with saliva, and a foul smell emanates from its anal glands. When opossums don't faint in these situations, they may instead react defensively by hissing, squawking, and baring their teeth. They have fifty teeth, more than any other mammal in North America.

Virginia opossum

Opossums have an impressive immune system that usually protects them against rabies and even venom from poisonous snakes. Despite this, however, they have an unusually short life expectancy for animals of their size—only one to two years in the wild. Even in captivity, they rarely live longer than four years. Some species of Australian possums, in contrast, live up to eleven years. In the wild, Virginia opossums are killed by dogs, cats, birds of prey, and cars.

Below is a juvenile **Eastern cottontail rabbit** eating a leaf of a lily outside my dining-room window. These animals are named for their fluffy white tails. Juveniles have a characteristic vertical white mark on their forehead, shown in the photograph below. Kits leave their nest (lined with grass and their mother's fur) by the time they are three weeks old, when they measure only four to five inches in length. Adults can grow to eighteen inches.

Juvenile Eastern cottontail rabbit

Note that hares and rabbits are not the same. Hares have much longer ears and do not dig burrows. Also, hares are born with fur, whereas rabbits are born naked. Cottontails typically live less than three years in the wild, although in captivity they may live as long as eight years.

North American raccoons (also called simply "raccoons") are common visitors to my bird feeders. When I type "Ohio raccoons" into Google to search for information, the first web site I encounter has a title of "Nuisance Species: How to deal with them – Ohio Department of Natural Resources." Despite being labeled as a nuisance, raccoons play a beneficial role by eating wasps (a single raccoon may consume an entire wasp's nest, including larvae) and by preventing the spread of poison ivy, by eating the berries.

Raccoons are found only in North America and are related to pandas. They typically live in found dens (e.g., hollows of trees, caves, or burrows) near a source of water. Like opossums, they are omnivores.

North American raccoon cub sitting in a flower-pot saucer

North American raccoon

North American raccoon

Raccoons are skillful climbers and can climb down trees headfirst by turning their hind feet 180 degrees. They are also resilient and may walk away uninjured after a forty-foot fall.

In the winter raccoons do not hibernate but sometimes remain in their dens for weeks at a time during severe weather. In the wild they have a life expectancy of only two to three years but rarely can live for up to sixteen years. In captivity they can live for more than twenty years.

Raccoons are fond of sunflower seeds and suet, and although they're normally nocturnal, they often come to my deck an hour or more before sunset to eat seeds and scoop out suet with their dexterous hands. Their hands resemble ours in appearance and functionality; they can open jars, turn doorknobs, and undo window latches.

Gray squirrels are also fond of the sunflower seeds and suet I put out for the birds, and they are particularly fond of raw peanuts. Some people scatter raw peanuts around their yard to keep squirrels away from bird feeders, and sometimes that works, although it requires a fair number of peanuts.

Gray squirrels

Unlike chipmunks, squirrels remain active in the winter, as shown on the previous page. The gray squirrel is one of four species of squirrels in Ohio, including fox, red, and flying squirrels. Gray squirrels are beneficial in the spreading of acorns, nuts, and seeds that give new growth to forests.

As their name implies, gray squirrels are predominantly gray, but they have a rusty orange coloration on the tips of their fur, and this becomes more apparent in the summer. They also typically have a light yellowish eye ring, and tan fur on the backs of their ears that becomes whiter in the winter. A black or melanistic form of this squirrel, native to Canada, can be found in Kent, Ohio, where I grew up. That variety of squirrel was brought to Kent in 1961 by a biology professor at Kent State University, and ten were released illegally into the wild.

Gray squirrels are excellent climbers, and like raccoons, they can climb headfirst down a tree. They do this by rotating their hind feet 180 degrees to allow their claws to dig into bark and grip against gravity.

All squirrels hoard and cache food. When they think they're being watched, they sometimes pretend to bury food, by digging a hole and making the motions of placing food in it (but hiding the food in their mouth), and then covering the hole.

Squirrels communicate both verbally with squeaks and nonverbally by posturing, including tail movements. They use nonverbal communication more often in noisy environments like urban areas.

Gray squirrels eat mostly seeds, acorns, nuts, berries, mushrooms, and tree bark. Rarely they eat insects and small animals, including bird eggs and chicks, when food is scarce. Therefore, feeding squirrels serves to protect birds.

Ohio was ninety-five percent covered by forests at the time it was first settled, an ideal habitat for squirrels, and gray squirrels were so numerous that people were required to hunt them in the early 1800s as part of paying taxes. Massive hunts for more than sixty years during the 1800s, along with extensive deforestation, resulted in a major decline in the population. In one hunt, a single hunter reportedly killed 160 squirrels in one day.

Gray squirrels can live up to sixteen years, but their life expectancy is only one year in Ohio. Some are killed by hunters, but many more are killed by cars and power lines. Others are preyed upon by dogs and cats. In the country, most die primarily because of a lack of food coupled with severe weather.

Squirrels can often be hand fed in areas where people don't harass them. When my wife and I visit Key Largo where we were married many years ago, the squirrels where we stay are so friendly that they hop onto a chaise with us and sit in our lap if we have something to feed them. On my back deck, they often go onto the gas grill only a foot from the window where I photograph birds, and they watch me while they eat peanuts I set out for them.

Taking Photographs and Providing a Safe Environment for Birds

Photographing birds is easier with good equipment, but good equipment isn't essential. Some of the best landscape and wildlife photographs I've taken were with a fully manual camera I purchased on a tight budget in college. I used that same camera for about twenty years, then switched to digital.

For all of the photographs in this book, I used a Nikon D3X and either an 80 – 400 mm or a 50 – 500 mm lens with vibration reduction. As I mentioned previously, in addition to not using a tripod, I did not use any special filters, not even a polarized filter, and I did not use a flash to photograph any of the birds. Flashes tend to enhance the quality of many images, but they also startle most animals and cause temporary impairment of vision at night, which renders them more vulnerable to predators. Even though I used a zoom lens, every species of bird that I saw, at one time or another, came within fifteen feet of me, and most within ten feet. Despite that, I took many of the photographs from farther away to show the birds in trees beyond my deck or in other parts of the yard seen through other windows. Much of what I saw was considerably more impressive than what I photographed, like the Cooper's hawk that twice landed on my deck, roughly ten feet from where I stood. Both times it happened too quickly for me to take a snapshot.

To get high-quality photographs of birds for this book, I cleaned my windows whenever they got significantly dirty. That varied from every day or two to every few weeks. I cleaned only part of them because birds are less likely to fly into a dirty window. First I removed a screen from one of several windows overlooking my back deck, but because of the risk of birds flying into the glass, my wife and I applied decals there, and to other glass windows and doors (although admittedly not to the windows in the dining room on the other side of the house). For decals to be effective, you should apply as many as possible, separated by as little space as possible. Sticking one decal in the center of a window is only marginally better than using no decals at all. You should also avoid putting indoor plants near windows without screens; some birds may try to land on the plant, not realizing a pane of glass separates them from it. If you have blinds or curtains, consider closing them when you aren't home.

When I take photographs through windows, I try to get as close to the window as possible. Sometimes I'll touch the rim of the lens to the glass, and that can help steady the camera for slow shutter speeds in low-light conditions. I photographed the closeup of the adult raccoon at 1/80 second using a focal length of 500 mm, and I photographed the raccoon cub sitting in the flower-pot saucer at 1/13 second using a focal length of 56 mm. As a general rule for a camera and lens without vibration reduction, the shutter speed should be at least as fast as the reciprocal of the focal length. That means for a 500 mm lens, the shutter speed should ideally be 1/500 second or faster to obtain a sharp image. Vibration reduction in a lens helps considerably, and steady hands are essential if you don't use a tripod. Sometimes I'll intentionally underexpose a picture to increase the shutter speed, compromising on the lighting to avoid noticeable blurring. I did that when photographing the scarlet tanager. I would rather have a slightly dark and grainy image with no evidence of camera motion than a blurry picture with optimal lighting.

For this project, I hung feeders on my back deck approximately ten to twenty feet from the window where I most frequently took photographs. I subsequently learned that feeders should ideally be either less than three feet or more than thirty feet from windows. Birds within three feet of windows are less likely to gather enough speed to kill themselves in a collision, and birds more than thirty feet away are less likely to see reflections that confuse them.

I put additional feeders on the ground under the deck for squirrels and chipmunks, but I avoid putting seeds directly on the ground. According to the Massachusetts Audubon Society, salmonella bacteria may contaminate seeds that soak up moisture from the ground, and it can readily spread from one bird to another through droppings. To minimize the likelihood of having this happen, I try to keep the feeding areas clean, including anywhere that birds might land.

Feeders should be cleaned at least every two to four weeks. The Massachusetts Audubon Society recommends soaking feeders in one part bleach to nine parts water for two or three minutes, then scrubbing, rinsing, and air drying. I change the water in bird baths and other watering containers every two or three days not only to provide clean water for the birds but also to prevent mosquitos from breeding. Recently I purchased a heated bird bath to keep water from freezing in the winter.

An adequate number of feeders should be used to prevent birds from jostling one another, to lessen the likelihood of spreading diseases by direct contact. House finches (and less commonly American goldfinches and downy woodpeckers) are susceptible to an eye infection that causes crusting and swelling and may cause blindness. This infection—mycobacterium gallisepticum—is spread by direct contact with other infected birds. It also infects chickens and turkeys.

I use several feeders, and I put all of them at the back of the house so I can fill or empty them without having to walk around much in the rain or snow. The back of my house happens to be a northern exposure, which means the sun is never directly behind the birds. When I take photographs of hummingbirds on the honeysuckle bush, I'm facing west, so I take all of those pictures in the morning or early afternoon. In general, pictures look better when the sun is low behind you rather than behind the subject you're photographing. During the middle of the afternoon, overcast days usually result in a better image because the contrast of sunlight and shadows is less problematic. Also, pictures usually look better when birds are on a branch rather than a feeder. Sometimes I'll tape branches to plant hangers, to encourage birds to land on something that appears more natural, and in the summer my wife puts a variety of plants and small trees on the back deck.

The National Audubon Society has a web site with information about creating a safe and healthful environment for backyard birds (http://web4.audubon.org/bird/at_home/Healthy_Yard.html), as well as tips about how to reduce the risk of birds colliding with windows (http://web4.audubon.org/bird/at_home/SafeWindows.html). The U.S. Fish and Wildlife Service estimates that as many as a billion birds in the U.S. die each year from these collisions. The danger is also present at night, especially from taller buildings when lights are left on. During nighttime migrations in severe weather, hundreds of birds may be killed in a single night by collisions with windows in a single building. Simply turning off bright lights and closing blinds can reduce bird deaths from nighttime collisions by more than 80%.

The National Audubon Society also recommends keeping cats indoors—cats kill more than a hundred million birds annually in the U.S.—and it recommends replacing areas of grass with alternative plants. If every homeowner in the U.S. replaced just one square yard of grass with flowers or other ground cover, that would eliminate an estimated 60,000 tons of grass clippings from landfills and would provide more than 10,000 acres of better habitat for wildlife.

Parting Words

The best way to attract most birds is to grow native plants that they like and to provide supplemental seeds, suet, and water. Also, birds feel less threatened when they aren't as exposed (e.g., on an open deck), and they're more visually appealing with plants around them. If you provide an environment that feels safe to them, they will regularly visit your plants and feeders.

For years I used windows just to let in light. Now I spend time looking through the glass. I hope you'll encourage others to do the same, to take an interest in their own backyards. No doubt they'll see more than they expect.